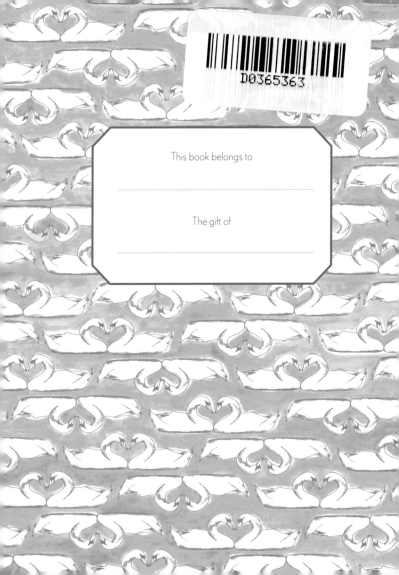

This book belongs to

....

The gift of

....

THE BOOK of LOVE

K.C. Jones
Illustrations by Diva Pyari

CHRONICLE BOOKS
SAN FRANCISCO

Text © 2010 by Chronicle Books LLC.
Illustrations © 2010 by Diva Pyari.
All rights reserved.
No part of this book may be reproduced in any form without
written permission from the publisher.

Library of Congress Cataloging-in-Publication Data:
Jones, K. C.
The book of love / K.C. Jones ; illustrations by Diva Pyari.
p. cm.
ISBN 978-0-8118-7720-6
1. Love–Miscellanea. I. Title.
GT2600.J66 2010
808.8'03543–dc22
2010004171

Manufactured in China

Designed by Sarah Pulver
Text by K.C. Jones

10 9 8 7 6 5 4 3 2

Chronicle Books LLC
680 Second Street
San Francisco, California 94107
www.chroniclebooks.com

CONTENTS

THERE IS ONLY ONE

HAPPINESS IN LIFE,

TO LOVE AND BE LOVED.

—GEORGE SAND

INTRODUCTION

*A*h, to be in love! It is a state many aspire to. But love is elusive; it cannot be easily drawn in or tempted. Luckily, love has a long history. For thousands of years, divine arts like astrology and numerology have pointed to what makes a good match. Time-honored rituals have created love where none existed before. Tokens of love have helped romance bloom. Love potions and aphrodisiacs have inflamed passion. And words of love, in all languages, have warmed hearts and drawn couples together.

Turn the page, fair reader, and learn how to make love come to you.

Life has taught us
that love does not
consist of gazing
at each other,
but looking outward
in the same direction.

Antoine de Saint-Exupéry

LOVE *matches*

Being in love is something we all covet. But being in
love with the *right* person is even rarer and more special.
Use this chapter to find your perfect match.

WHAT'S YOUR SIGN?

The month and day you were born can predict your behavior when it comes to love. Astrology can also tell which signs are good love matches for you—and which ones you should avoid.

If your birthday falls on or between these dates . . . *

Your astrological sign is . . .

March 22–April 21	Aries
April 22–May 21	Taurus
May 22–June 21	Gemini
June 22–July 21	Cancer
July 22–August 21	Leo
August 22–September 21	Virgo
September 22–October 21	Libra
October 22–November 21	Scorpio
November 22–December 21	Sagittarius
December 22–January 21	Capricorn
January 22–February 21	Aquarius
February 22–March 21	Pisces

* If your birthday is two to three days from the beginning or end of a date range, you are "on the cusp," meaning that you may also display characteristics of the sign that precedes or follows the sign you fall under, as well as the characteristics of your own sign.

THE SIGNS IN LOVE

ARIES

Most Compatible with: Leo, Sagittarius
Least Compatible with: Cancer, Libra, Capricorn

Aries in love: Aries, in love you are charming and often irresistible—you draw lovers to you with little effort. You can be quick to anger but also express warm feelings easily.

If you love an Aries: Keep in mind that Aries enjoys the chase, and sometimes sees love as a game or a conquest. Do not become attached too quickly. Once your Aries has committed, however, the relationship will be forever interesting, fresh, and passionate.

TAURUS

Most Compatible with: Virgo, Capricorn
Least Compatible with: Leo, Scorpio, Aquarius

Taurus in love: Taurus, you enjoy life's simple pleasures—displays of materialism are not for you. When it comes to love, quiet nights at home are better than fancy dinners out.

If you love a Taurus: Your mate will be easygoing, straightforward, stable, and reliable. Expect undying loyalty—but know that you will have to return that loyalty for the relationship to work.

GEMINI

Most Compatible with: Libra, Aquarius
Least Compatible with: Virgo, Sagittarius, Pisces

Gemini in love: Your relationships are never boring, Gemini. And communication is one of your strong points. You wear your heart on your sleeve and your lovers almost always know where they stand.

If you love a Gemini: Expect lots of spontaneity, which makes for a lively life. But if you seek stability and deep emotional support, Gemini may not be able to provide it.

CANCER

Most Compatible with: Scorpio, Pisces
Least Compatible with: Aries, Libra, Capricorn

Cancer in love: Cancer, you are patient and kind when it comes to love. And your keen intuition makes you an empathetic partner.

If you love a Cancer: The typical Cancer is unfailingly generous and protective; you must be open to this caretaking. If you pride yourself on your independent nature, you and Cancer will not be a match.

LEO

Most Compatible with: Aries, Sagittarius
Least Compatible with: Taurus, Scorpio, Aquarius

Leo in love: When you fall in love, Leo, you fall hard. You love to lavish affection and gifts on your beloved, provided that person gives you the attention you also crave.

If you love a Leo: Your Leo is romantic, idealistic, and loyal once in the right relationship. However, Leo also has a dominant personality, so you must be open to relinquishing the spotlight every now and again.

VIRGO

Most Compatible with: Taurus, Capricorn
Least Compatible with: Gemini, Sagittarius, Pisces

Virgo in love: Virgo, you are selective and slow to trust when it comes to love; this stems from an underlying vulnerability. But once you find your match, your affections are always genuine.

If you love a Virgo: Your Virgo is nurturing and supportive and handles adversity well. Virgo is just the person you want around when times get tough.

LIBRA

Most Compatible with: Gemini, Aquarius
Least Compatible with: Aries, Cancer, Capricorn

Libra in love: Libra, many who meet you are drawn to you, though your true goal is to find that one person who will complete you. Your analytical nature can turn this goal into a lifelong quest.

If you love a Libra: Decisiveness is not your Libra's strong suit, so it would serve you well to exercise patience. However, Libra strives for harmony in love, so you will rarely argue.

SCORPIO

Most Compatible with: Cancer, Pisces
Least Compatible with: Taurus, Leo, Aquarius

Scorpio in love: You are among the most passionate signs when it comes to love, Scorpio. However, trust is another matter. Work on this if you want to build long-term relationships.

If you love a Scorpio: Your Scorpio will be unendingly faithful and committed, but also prone to jealousy. And if you try and control Scorpio, you will be stung.

SAGITTARIUS

Most Compatible with: Aries, Leo
Least Compatible with: Gemini, Virgo, Pisces

Sagittarius in love: You are honest and forthright at all costs, Sagittarius, so you must have a partner who does not need things sugar-coated. An ideal companion will be as independent as you are.

If you love a Sagittarius: Sagittarius's sense of humor and fun is unparalleled, and you will never be bored. But be careful not to be at all possessive, or your Sagittarius will rebel.

CAPRICORN

Most Compatible with: Taurus, Virgo
Least Compatible with: Aries, Cancer, Libra

Capricorn in love: Capricorn, you thrive on committed relationships and take your responsibility as one half of a couple very seriously. You should be with a mate who is as practical, reliable, and stable as you are.

If you love a Capricorn: Take care to tell Capricorn how you feel on a regular basis; this sign fears rejection and will open up slowly if not encouraged. If you are expressive, you will find Capricorn surprisingly passionate.

AQUARIUS

Most Compatible with: Gemini, Libra
Least Compatible with: Taurus, Leo, Scorpio

Aquarius in love: Physical appearance is not the most important thing to you in love, Aquarius; you prefer companions who interest you intellectually. But you do need a mate who will let you keep some measure of independence.

If you love an Aquarius: Aquarius seeks out the unconventional when it comes to love, so you needn't be ashamed of your quirks. And your Aquarius will be loyal to a fault.

PISCES

Most Compatible with: Cancer, Scorpio
Least Compatible with: Gemini, Virgo, Sagittarius

Pisces in love: Pisces, you possess deep wells of compassion and caring, and will go above and beyond to avoid hurting your mate. Be careful not to keep secrets just to maintain harmony in the relationship.

If you love a Pisces: Pisces is open-minded and tolerant, so you can tell your darkest secrets without fear of rejection. Pisces has a need to help others, and will be there for you through thick and thin.

THE CHINESE ZODIAC

Using the Chinese Zodiac (an astrological system based on birth year) is another way to divine who your best love matches will be—and which signs are not a good fit. To determine which animal represents you, look for your birth year in the chart. The Chinese calendar is lunar, so if you were born in January or early February, look to the year prior to your birth year.

IF YOU WERE BORN IN...	YOUR ZODIAC ANIMAL IS...
1912, 1924, 1936, 1948, 1960, 1972, 1984, 1996, 2008	RAT
1913, 1925, 1937, 1949, 1961, 1973, 1985, 1997, 2009	OX
1914, 1926, 1938, 1950, 1962, 1974, 1986, 1998, 2010	TIGER
1915, 1927, 1939, 1951, 1963, 1975, 1987, 1999, 2011	RABBIT
1916, 1928, 1940, 1952, 1964, 1976, 1988, 2000, 2012	DRAGON
1917, 1929, 1941, 1953, 1965, 1977, 1989, 2001, 2013	SNAKE
1918, 1930, 1942, 1954, 1966, 1978, 1990, 2002, 2014	HORSE
1919, 1931, 1943, 1955, 1967, 1979, 1991, 2003, 2015	SHEEP*
1920, 1932, 1944, 1956, 1968, 1980, 1992, 2004, 2016	MONKEY
1921, 1933, 1945, 1957, 1969, 1981, 1993, 2005, 2017	ROOSTER
1922, 1934, 1946, 1958, 1970, 1982, 1994, 2006, 2018	DOG
1923, 1935, 1947, 1959, 1971, 1983, 1995, 2007, 2019	PIG

* *sometimes also referred to as Ram or Goat*

THE SIGNS IN LOVE

RAT

Most Compatible with: Dragon and Monkey
Least Compatible with: Horse

Rat in love: In love, you are charming and funny, but you can also be selfish. Work on giving more of yourself, and your relationship will thrive.

If you love a Rat: Rat is generous and kind but can have a short fuse when provoked.

OX

Most Compatible with: Snake, Rooster
Least Compatible with: Sheep

Ox in love: When it comes to love, Ox, you are protective of your mate. This is a good quality, as long as you take care not to be stifling.

If you love an Ox: Ox is patient, kind, and methodical in all he or she does—but can sometimes be egotistical.

TIGER

Most Compatible with: Horse, Dog
Least Compatible with: Monkey

Tiger in love: You are warm-hearted and passionate, and you love with great ardor. You will be happiest with a mate who shares your intensity.

If you love a Tiger: Tiger has great seductive powers, but can be moody at times.

RABBIT

Most Compatible with: Sheep, Pig
Least Compatible with: Rooster

Rabbit in love: Rabbit, your greatest love is for your home and family. You are the kindest and gentlest of all the animals, and you have the capacity to be a nurturing parent.

If you love a Rabbit: Your Rabbit is sincere and compassionate. However, he or she avoids conflict at all costs.

DRAGON

Most Compatible with: Snake, Rooster
Least Compatible with: Sheep

Dragon in love: The early phases of your love affairs are full of fireworks. But when the embers die down, you are tempted to move on. In doing so, you might miss the affection and companionship that comes with enduring love.

If you love a Dragon: Dragon is warm-hearted and charismatic but may also be egotistical.

SNAKE

Most Compatible with: Rooster, Ox
Least Compatible with: Pig

Snake in love: You are blessed with good looks, and so you attract romantic partners easily. However, you can be somewhat vain. Work to find beauty inside yourself as well.

If you love a Snake: Your Snake is intelligent and dedicated to work, and generous and charming. He or she can be jealous, however.

HORSE

Most Compatible with: Tiger, Dog
Least Compatible with: Rat

Horse in love: You are magnetic and draw love to you easily. Once in love, though, you can tend to be too self-reliant. To be successful in love, you will need to open up a bit.

If you love a Horse: Horse is caring, energetic, and adventurous, though may be impatient if his or her partner moves more slowly.

SHEEP

Most Compatible with: Rabbit, Pig
Least Compatible with: Ox

Sheep in love: Sheep, you are a nurturer when it comes to love and as such make a good romantic partner. However, you expect to be cared for in return, and you can be oversensitive if you feel you are being neglected.

If you love a Sheep: Your Sheep is an extremely creative thinker, but along with these creative energies he or she sometimes possesses an insecurity that you will need to soothe.

MONKEY

Most Compatible with: Dragon, Rat
Least Compatible with: Tiger

Monkey in love: Monkey, you are fun-loving and draw love to you easily. But long-term relationships are not your forte. If you want a partner for life, you will need to work on your staying power.

If you love a Monkey: Monkey is a good listener, and empathetic, but often puts him- or herself above others when it comes to love.

ROOSTER

Most Compatible with: Snake, Ox
Least Compatible with: Rabbit

Rooster in love: In love you are straightforward and direct. You will make a good match with someone who is similar in nature to you.

If you love a Rooster: Rooster is an analytical, shrewd sign, and is usually in good shape when it comes to financial affairs. However, he or she knows it, so be prepared for some boasting.

DOG

Most compatible with: Tiger, Horse
Least compatible with: Dragon

Dog in love: Though it may be hard for you to find a suitable mate, once you do, it will prove to be a faithful and loyal union.

If you love a Dog: Your Dog will be committed to you until the end but will also be critical of you at times.

PIG

Most Compatible with: Sheep, Rabbit
Least Compatible with: Pig

Pig in love: You do not make things complicated when it comes to love—with you, what you see is what you get. Because of this, you will make a solid lifelong companion once you find the right mate.

If you love a Pig: Your Pig is a perfectionist but will not make you feel like you need to be one, too—this sign is very tolerant of others' differences.

BY THE NUMBERS

The science of numerology is another way to make a good love match. To use it, you must determine both a number for yourself and for your mate (or desired mate), based on your full names.

Refer to the chart below—you will see that each number, 1 through 9, has corresponding letters beneath it.

1	2	3	4	5	6	7	8	9
A	B	C	D	E	F	G	H	I
J	K	L	M	N	O	P	Q	R
S	T	U	V	W	X	Y	Z	

Write out your full name (including middle name).

For example,

MARY CLARA SMITH

Now, using the chart, place corresponding numbers under each letter.

MARY CLARA SMITH
4 197 33191 14928

Now add the numbers for each of the names together.
If the result is a 2-digit number, add those numbers together.

$4+1+9+7 = 21 \rightarrow 2+1 = 3$

$3+3+1+9+1 = 17 \rightarrow 1+7 = 8$

$1+4+9+2+8 = 24 \rightarrow 2+4 = 6$

Finally, add those three numbers together. Again, if the result is 2 digits, add those digits so the result is a 1-digit number—unless the result is 11 or 22. Those numbers are master numbers that have special significance as revealed, along with the other numbers' meanings, on the following page.

$3+8+6=17 \rightarrow 1+7=8$

8 is the result.

What do the numbers mean?

1 → Creative, independent, original, adventurous, yet egotistical

2 → Empathetic, diplomatic, sensitive, intuitive, cautious, yet codependent

3 → Artistic, enthusiastic, visionary, optimistic, sociable, yet superficial and wasteful

4 → Organized, efficient, practical, loyal, serious, yet rigid

5 → Creative, inventive, free-spirited, adaptable, yet volatile

6 → Responsible, understanding, loving, passionate, harmonious, yet jealous

7 → Intuitive, spiritual, wise, analytical, yet critical and isolated

8 → Powerful, decisive, authoritative, organized, yet materialistic

9 → Compassionate, generous, romantic, imaginative, devoted, yet overemotional

11 → Creative, idealistic, inventive, wise, yet insensitive. An 11 can also have characteristics of a 2, since 1+1 = 2.

22 → Innovative, driven, practical, masterful, yet harsh. A 22 can also have characteristics of a 4, since 2+2 = 4.

Now that you understand what numerology says about you as an individual, you can apply its powers to work for your relationship. Determine the number that applies to your beloved, and then

	1	2	3	4
1	Competitive yet passionate	Must work to keep romance alive	A complementary match	A struggle for control
2	Must work to keep romance alive	Strong mutual respect	Powerful chemistry	Stable and long-lasting
3	A complementary match	Powerful chemistry	An extremely social pairing	Need to give each other breathing room
4	A struggle for control	Stable and long-lasting	Need to give each other breathing room	Stable if spontaneity remains
5	Independence and passion	Needs constant work	Keep an eye on life's details	Work on communication skills
6	Work on mutual respect and support	Caring, family-oriented	A stable yet creative and nurturing duo	A happy home life awaits
7	Motivated and passionate	A difficult pairing	Opposites attract!	Devoted and true, but lacking passion
8	A happy match, if romance is the priority	A relationship with staying power	Remember to enjoy each other	Hard work leads to security
9	Compatible despite differences	Show love, and the passion will grow	Share the spotlight	Focus on your commonalities, not your differences

look to the table below to find the intersection of your two numbers. (If you are an 11, use 2 as your number; if you are a 22, use 4.)

5	6	7	8	9
Independence and passion	Work on mutual respect and support	Motivated and passionate	A happy match, if romance is the priority	Compatible despite differences
Needs constant work	Caring, family-oriented	A difficult pairing	A relationship with staying power	Show love, and the passion will grow
Keep an eye on life's details	A stable yet creative and nurturing duo	Opposites attract!	Remember to enjoy each other	Share the spotlight
Work on communication skills	A happy home life awaits	Devoted and true, but lacking passion	Hard work leads to security	Focus on your commonalities, not your differences
Adventure and passion, if you can keep jealousy in check	Compromise is the key to happiness	A true intellectual match	Always make plans, and see the big picture	Make time for love
Compromise is the key to happiness	Family comes first	Control issues lie in your path	Honesty and openness are hallmarks	Mutual admiration makes for stability
A true intellectual match	Control issues lie in your path	Easy and placid	Sparks fly in the bedroom—but watch your fiery tempers	A true spiritual connection
Always make plans, and see the big picture	Honesty and openness are hallmarks	Sparks fly in the bedroom—but watch your fiery tempers	A passionate match, if you remember to communicate	Know yourselves well and harmony will follow
Make time for love	Mutual admiration makes for stability	A true spiritual connection	Know yourselves well and harmony will follow	A bond characterized by selflessness

WHAT'S IN A PALM?

Palmistry, or palm reading, is the study of foretelling future life events based on the lines in a person's hand.

To read a palm for love, you must understand the different lines present in every person's hand. Which palm you read also makes a difference; in general, the palm of a person's dominant hand can tell you about current and actual behavior, while the palm of the nondominant hand represents potential. The more different the two palms, the more the subject has strived to change his or her ways or fulfill his or her potential.

There are four main shapes of the hand, and these correspond to the four elements: Earth, Air, Fire, and Water.

Earth: The palm is square, the fingers are short, and the lines are deep. In love, Earths are steadfast, reliable, and stable.

Air: The palm is square or slightly rectangular, with long fingers, and thin lines. In love, these people believe a mental and spiritual connection is most important.

Fire: These people have long palms but short fingers, and more lines in their palms than other people. In love, they are confident, optimistic leaders.

Water: Both the palm and the fingers are long. The palm lines are very fine and indistinct. In love, these people are sensitive and caring, but vulnerable and naïve.

The thumb can also signify a person's love behavior. A relatively long thumb shows a faithful character when it comes to love.

A thumb that narrows before meeting the hand symbolizes a person who is tactful and kind in love.

There are particular and specific lines on the palm that speak directly to a person's love habits and tendencies.

The palm consists of major lines, minor lines, and secondary lines. In general, the more fine lines on a palm, the more sensitive, intuitive, complex, and vulnerable a person is in love. A palm that has fewer fine lines most likely belongs to a straightforward person who thrives on directness and will tell his or her lover like it is.

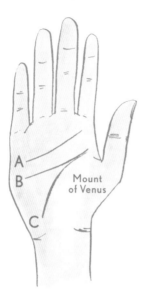

Mount
of Venus

A........the heart line
B........the head line
C........the life line

The major horizontal line at the top of the palm is the **Heart Line**
(line A on the diagram), which rules love and the emotions. The
higher the Heart Line is (the closer to the top of the palm), the
more passion its owner possesses. Beware, however, for a high
Heart Line can also symbolize a tendency toward jealousy.

An upwardly curved Heart Line (pointing toward the
index finger) can stand for a person who is expressive and
affectionate, while a straighter Heart Line generally means a
more stoic individual who can be closed off in love.

The Heart Line can also speak to love history and future. The
more lines that cross and break the Heart Line, the more
sadness in love that person will experience.

The horizontal line in the middle of the palm *(line B)* is called the **Head Line**, which governs intelligence but can also provide insight into love. The same goes for the Life Line, which runs from the base of the palm upward toward the thumb and index finger *(line C)*. If the Head Line and the Life Line meet, or come close together, this indicates a person who is cautious when it comes to love. If the two lines diverge, it is likely that the palm's owner takes more risks in love.

The place where the Life Line exits the palm (between the thumb and index finger) speaks to the level of generosity a person displays in a love relationship: closer to the index finger means more generous, closer to the thumb means less generous.

Horizontal lines above the Heart Line are called **Lines of Attachment**. One long and deep line forecasts a long and happy love commitment; several lines represent shorter, less intense relationships.

The **Mount of Venus** is the fleshy part of the palm between the thumb and the Life Line. If, when squeezed, it is more firm, this signifies a strong sexual vitality; if it is more loose and flabby, the person's sexual appetite may be low.

Lines on the Mount of Venus indicate other aspects of love. A person with prominent horizontal lines in this area has a magnetic power over lovers, while a grid of horizontal and vertical lines suggests fickleness in love. Lines that form a triangle indicate a person who will struggle with fidelity.

i carry your heart

(i carry it in my heart)

~ e. e. cummings

LOVE
charms

While there is no surefire way to ensure that you will fall
in love precisely when you want, there are many time-tested
charms, rituals, and omens that can point the way.
Pay attention to them, and love will likely follow.

SIGNS YOU WILL SOON FALL IN LOVE OR MARRY

- If you stumble while climbing a flight of stairs. (Stumbling while descending stairs does not have the same effect, and can be dangerous! Keep your hand on the banister at all times.)

- If you see stockings hanging on a washing line curl around each other. If the washing line is your own, the portent is even stronger. If the stockings are already curled together when you come upon them, love will come but not as quickly as if you see the curling happen.

- If you hear a bird call from the east. On the other hand, a cricket chirping from the east means an old lover is not far away.

- On St. George's Day (April 23), go into a field or meadow with at least four other single women and one white dog. Blindfold the dog, and then place yourselves in a circle around the field, equidistant from the dog. The first woman the dog touches will be married within the year.

- If a man wipes his hands on your apron he'll soon fall in love with you. Attempts to precipitate this by offering your apron to the man may backfire. He must reach for the apron on his own!

- On New Year's Eve, throw your shoe or boot into a willow tree. If it catches in the branches, you will be married within the year. You may make nine attempts. Any more than that and you will end up an old maid.

- If you find bubbles floating in your noncarbonated drink, love is coming soon. If the bubbles are touching the rim of the glass it means that with love will also come wealth!

- If two spoons are placed by accident on one saucer, it foretells marriage within the year for the person using the saucer.

DREAMS OF LOVE

The following dreams mean that love will soon enter your life:

- If you dream of making a bed

- If you dream of a tortoiseshell cat

- If you dream of eating honey

- If you dream of taking a bath (dreaming of swimming does not hold the same meaning)

If you wish to dream of love, do these things:

- Sprinkle one sprig of rosemary and one sprig of thyme with water, and place the sprigs in a pair of your finest shoes. Prop the shoes at the end of your bed. Or, if you do not have herbs on hand, simply place the heel of the left shoe against the instep of the right shoe and place them at the foot of the bed.

- Go to sleep with your nightgown turned inside out.

- Pin a bay leaf to each corner of your pillow before sleeping on it.

- Eat one half of an apple before midnight, and the other half after midnight. Stand in the light of the moon while doing so for best results.

- Sleep with any of the following things under your pillow:
  - A mirror
  - Three small stones gathered from beside a body of water
  - A small piece of cake that has been passed through a gold ring
  - A silver spoon

To Learn Who Your Future Love Is

- If your right eye itches and you do not scratch it, you'll soon see your true love, whether in a vision or in reality. If you scratch the itch, however, you'll scratch the vision away and the love will not come to fruition.

- Peel an apple in one long strip. Drop the peel into a large bowl of water. Whatever letter the peel forms is the initial of your future love.

To Create Love

- ❦ Cleave a strawberry in half. Eat one half and give the other half to the object of your affection. If he eats it in your presence, he will fall in love with you.

- ❦ While thinking of the person you want to make yours, roll a ring away from you. If it falls to the right, it will happen; to the left, it is not meant to be.

- ❦ Rub the headboard of your bed with the skin of a lemon before you retire for the night, all the while thinking of the person you want to make your beloved.

- ❦ Find a donkey, horse, or mule with long ears. Look it in the eye and ask it if you will fall in love soon. If the animal moves its head, the answer is yes. If only its ears move, the outcome is unclear. If it does not move at all, the answer is no.

- ❦ Count nine stars on each of nine consecutive nights. (If the night is overcast and stars are obscured, you must start the count over.) On the morning of the tenth day, the first single man you see will be yours, if you want him.

- ❦ If you find a piece of red cloth or ribbon on the ground, this signifies good luck in love will come to you soon. However, you must pick up the red item while wishing for love and carry it with you at all times in order for the portent to come true. (A found yellow ribbon means friendship will soon come; a white ribbon signifies that the finder will soon make peace with an enemy.)

- Cut an apple in half with a sharp knife. If you can do this without cutting through any of the seeds inside the apple, you will fall in love soon.

- Bake a cake that contains apples and place a small piece of it on a frequently traveled pathway. Watch and wait. If the first person to step on the cake is a woman, your future husband will be an older man or one who has already been married; if a man steps on the cake, your husband will be a young man.

- To attract love, place one pinch each of parsley, thyme, and rosemary on a small piece of aluminum foil. Fold the foil up into a small bundle, keeping the herbs safe inside. Wear this bundle close to your heart for ten days.

To Keep Love Once You Have It

- Tie a strand of your hair to that of your lover's with a red ribbon and wear it near your heart. He will never stray.

- Hold a freshly picked sprig of mint in your palm and have your lover clasp his hand to yours. Hold your hands together, without speaking, until the mint is warm.

- Present your love with a piece of sweet butter on a new dish while you are sitting outdoors (a picnic is a perfect excuse!).

- Sit with your lover on a Friday and share wine from the same glass, while summoning the spirit of Aphrodite and asking her to bless your love. If you do not finish the wine, pour it on the ground, not down the drain.

- To seal a new love, have your first kiss take place during a new moon. Even better if it happens outside, under the moon.

- Find a laurel twig or branch and break it in half as evenly as you can. Keep one half for yourself and give the other half to your love. As long as you hold on to your halves, both of you will be always faithful.

- Set a table for your love, and place two fish and a glass of brandy atop it. If your love reaches first for the fish, you will be forever happy. If he or she reaches for the brandy, trouble lies ahead.

- Never look at the full moon together through a window or a looking-glass; this is bad luck for love.

- Take care to never catch on fire the hair of your love; this will extinguish the passion in the relationship immediately.

RITUALS MEN CAN
PERFORM TO WOO WOMEN

- If a man finds willow twigs or branches that have grown into a knot, he should clip the knot from the tree, tie it up in a handkerchief, and hide it in the bed of the woman he desires. If she does not find it within a fortnight, she will fall in love with him.

- A man should pluck a blade of grass from an open field and, holding it, recite this charm, once facing east and once facing west:

  Where the sun goes up
  Shall my love be by me
  Where the sun goes down
  There by her I will be.

  He should then cut the blade of grass up into tiny pieces and surreptitiously mix it with some food that the object of his desire will eat. If she ingests the grass, she will fall in love with him.

❦ At the break of dawn on a Friday, a single man should pluck the most beautiful apple from a tree and cut it in half. He should then tear a piece of paper in half and write his name on one half and his love's name on the other. He should affix the pieces of paper to the apple halves using pins made of myrtle wood, and then dry the apples in a low oven. Finally, he should place the apple half bearing his name under his love's pillow, and the half bearing his love's name under his own pillow, and wait for the magic to work.

HOW TO PUNISH
LOVERS WHO HAVE STRAYED

❦ Light a candle at midnight and while it burns, prick it three times with a knife or needle, thinking of your former lover and repeating

Thrice the candle's broke by me,
Thrice thy heart shall broken be.

This will ruin his or her current relationship.

❦ Grind the shell of a crab or lobster to a fine powder and mix some of it into food your ex-lover will be eating. This will make him or her pine for you always.

THE POWER OF THE MOON

Timing love rituals to coincide with the most fortuitous phases of the moon will give your chances an extra boost.

If the moon is waxing: This is a good time for relationships to begin.

If the moon is waning: Negative aspects in a relationship can be cured if worked on during this period.

If it is a full moon: This is a positive time for love and romance, especially in the daylight hours.

If it is a new moon: During this period, love and romance blossom best during the hours just around midnight.

LOVE RITUALS
FROM OTHER CULTURES

The Anglo-Saxon term *daes eage*, or "day's eye," later became the word "daisy," a flower that was believed to have forecasting powers. Victorian maids who had been jilted by their loves would pick a daisy and one by one, pluck off each of its petals, chanting "He loves me, he loves me not, he loves me. . . ." The phrase that was uttered during the plucking of the final petal was to be the true outcome.

In seventeenth-century England, eligible young girls would hold "silent suppers" on or around the summer solstice. These dinners would take place late at night and without any of the diners speaking to each other. Everything happened backwards: servants took plates from the kitchen to the table while walking backward, courses were eaten in reverse, and diners sat facing away from the table. Everyone sat in silence until the clock struck midnight, at which point each young girl was supposed to see the ghostly form of her future husband appearing in the room.

An Old English rhyme speaks to another love tradition. Two girls would go into the woods after dark. Each would hold one end of a leaf, and together they would recite:

> If I am to marry near,
> Let me hear a bird cry.
> If I am to marry far,
> Let me hear a cow low.
> If I am to single die,
> Let me hear a knocking by.

They would then wait patiently for one of these noises to occur—and thus their love fate was sealed!

In medieval times, single Romanian women sought to divine the origin of their future husbands by standing naked at midnight in the nearest lake or river. As the clock struck twelve, they would listen carefully for a dog's bark. They believed that the direction the bark came from would be the same direction the future suitor would come from.

FORTUITOUS TIMES TO FALL IN LOVE AND MARRY

The timing of particular love milestones can speak volumes. The following Old English rhymes propose good months and days to marry, what color to wear on the wedding day, and what days are luckiest for childbearing.

WHAT MONTH TO MARRY

Married when the year is new,
He'll be loving, kind, and true.
When February birds do mate
You wed nor dread your fate.
If you wed when March winds blow
Joy and sorrow both you'll know.
Marry in April when you can
Joy for maiden and the man.
Marry in the month of May
And you'll surely rue the day.
Marry when June roses grow
Over land and sea you'll go.
Those who in July do wed
Must labor for their daily bread.
Whoever wed in August be,
Many a change is sure to see.

Marry in September's shine,
Your living will be rich and fine;
If in October you do marry,
Love will come but riches tarry;
If you wed in bleak November,
Only joy will come, remember;
When December's showers fall fast,
Marry and true love will last.

··· ♡ ···

WHAT DAY TO MARRY

Monday for wealth,
Tuesday for health,
Wednesday the best day of all;
Thursday for crosses,
Friday for losses,
Saturday no luck at all.

WHAT TO WEAR TO MARRY

Married in White, you have chosen right

Married in Grey, you will go far away,

Married in Black, you will wish yourself back,

Married in Red, you will wish yourself dead,

Married in Green, ashamed to be seen,

Married in Blue, you will always be true,

Married in Pearl, you will live in a whirl,

Married in Yellow, ashamed of your fellow,

Married in Brown, you will live in the town,

Married in Pink, you spirit will sink.

WHEN TO BEAR CHILDREN

Monday's child is fair of face,
Tuesday's child is full of grace,
Wednesday's child is full of woe,
Thursday's child has far to go,
Friday's child is loving and giving,
Saturday's child works hard for a living,
But the child who is born on the Sabbath Day
Is bonny and blithe and good and gay.

READING THE LEAVES

Reading tea leaves, a practice called tasseography, is an ancient method of fortune-telling. The tea leaves can tell you what love is in store for you in the future.

To prepare the tea, you will need a teapot with a large spout, so the tea leaves can easily be poured along with the tea. You will also need white teacups and saucers (teacups that are colored obscure the tea leaf reading) and loose tea with large leaves (tea in tea bags is ground too finely for an accurate reading). Brew the tea to your liking in the pot and then pour it into teacups, without straining the leaves. Let the leaves settle to the bottom of the cup before drinking. Drink the tea until only a small bit of liquid remains in the bottom of the cup, about a half teaspoonful, along with the leaves.

To read the leaves, swirl the cup three times in a counter-clockwise direction. Turn the cup over onto the saucer carefully. Let all the liquid drain out for a minute or two; this is a necessary step, for it "sets" the leaves. Turn the cup right-side up and hold it by the handle. The leaves that remain inside hold your fortune! (Coffee grounds may also be read in this same manner, as in the Turkish tradition.)

To be an expert in tasseography, years of experience are needed, so divining the symbols inside your cup may be difficult if you are new to tea leaves. If you do not see any discernible forms while looking directly into your cup, squint into the cup instead. This will reduce the tea leaves to shapes and outlines and allow you to see more clearly.

What do the symbols represent for love? There are hundreds, even thousands, of possible tea-leaf forms, but here are some common examples:

Anchor: Your love life will have a pleasing constancy about it.

Angel: You will have good fortune in love and perhaps happiness greater than you could have ever dreamed. If the angel is in flight, the good fortune will come upon you soon.

Banner: You will marry a wealthy man. If you are already married, expect riches to come to your family.

Basket: A pregnancy is in your future.

Bottle: This signifies happy times ahead in love; the more bottles, the greater happiness.

Chain: You will become engaged or marry soon. But if the chain is broken, beware: your union may be a rocky one.

Church: This portends future ease in love.

Flowers: An especially fortuitous symbol. Seeing any type of flower in your tea leaves means you will have a happy and fulfilling marriage, and success in all areas of your life.

Eye: Seeing an eye signifies the love in your life will be deep and strong.

Ferns: The person you love will be dignified, honest, and steadfast.

Fish: A future lover will come to you from abroad. Or, if the fish is upside down, you will travel to him!

Frog: Success in love is foretold for you.

Kangaroo: Be on your guard, a rival will vie for your lover's attention.

Key: You will be financially successful, and your spouse will always be good to you.

Lighthouse: This signifies lifelong security in love.

Mushroom: Seeing the shape of a mushroom may mean that quarrels in love are ahead. It may even portend a broken engagement.

Pen: Marriage is on the horizon for you.

Pig: Your lover will be forever faithful.

Ring: A ring is a signifier of marriage. If it stands alone in the cup, the marriage will be happy; if the ring is crossed with other symbols, there is trouble ahead. And if the ring lies squarely in the bottom of the cup, the marriage will end.

Strawberries: Great pleasure in love will come to you.

Swan: You will be lucky throughout your life, but especially so in love.

Trees: Trees are a sign of happiness in love, as well as prosperity and good health.

Triangles: Good luck in love will come to you, though it will be when you least expect it.

On the whole, dark leaves and grounds represent men but can also stand for dark-haired people; lighter leaves and grounds represent women and fair-haired people.

It is also common for numbers and letters to appear in tea leaves. These elements should be read in conjunction with the other symbols around them. For example, a ring plus a letter may mean your future mate's name begins with that letter. If that cup also contains a number—for example, 3—it could mean it will be 3 days, or 3 months, or 3 years before your love fate is carried out.

Other combinations of tea leaves are rarer, but equally powerful:

Daffodils and a sun: Joy will come to you in the spring—perhaps an engagement or a marriage?

A sword and a chain: You will marry a soldier or policeman and live happily.

A sword, a ring, a human figure, and a toad: You will be separated by your lover due to the lies of malicious strangers.

A ladder, a ring, and a human figure: It will be through marriage that you fulfill your destiny.

A palm tree and water: You will travel with your love to a warm climate.

A pen, flowers, and a musical instrument: Your marriage will bring you immense happiness.

A bird, a trident, and a ring: You will be pursued by a stranger who will soon propose marriage—he may be a sailor or other seaman.

Flowers, a bird, a crescent moon, a ring: You will marry in the early spring.

Where the leaves sit in the cup is also an important predictor of fate. Shapes close to the handle mean outcomes will happen close to home. Shapes that point to the handle denote events that will happen in the future. And shapes that are closer to the rim of the cup mean events that will take place sooner than the events augured by the leaves near the bottom of the cup.

GODS, GODDESSES, AND SPIRITS OF LOVE

Summon these deities when you need a little help in love.

Aizen-Myo-o: Japanese (Buddhist) god of love

Aphrodite: Greek goddess of love

Branwyn: Celtic goddess of love, sexuality, and the ocean

Cupid: Roman god of love

Eros: Greek god of love

Erzulie: Voodoo goddess of love, passion, fertility, beauty, and sex

Freya: Norse goddess of love and beauty

Freyr: Norse god of fertility and success

Hathor: Egyptian goddess of love and joy

Inanna: Sumerian goddess of love and war

Ishtar: Babylonian goddess of love

Isis: Egyptian goddess of fertility, motherhood, and magic

Juno: Roman goddess of marriage and protector of
women in labor

Kama: Hindu god of love

Lakshmi: Hindu goddess of beauty and fertility

Oshun: Yoruban spirit-goddess of love, beauty, and intimacy

Radha: Hindu goddess of love

Tlazolteotl: Aztec goddess of love, fertility, sex, and childbirth

Venus: Roman goddess of love

Xochipilli: Aztec god of love

My bounty is as deep
as the sea,
My love as deep;
the more I give to thee,
The more I have,
for both are infinite.

~ William Shakespeare

LOVE tokens

Offering gifts to show one's love is an age-old practice.
In medieval Europe, suitors would bend copper coins and
give them to their sweethearts as a token of their love.
To return that love, women would carry the coins with them
and never spend them. Though the bent coins of today
often take the form of jewelry, flowers, and chocolates,
the sentiment behind them is no less meaningful.

THE MEANING OF FLOWERS

Flowers, plants, and herbs have meaning. When you give or receive flowers as gifts, keep in mind the sentiment they carry.

Acacia: secret love

Acorn: strength, fidelity, prosperity

Almond: hope

Alyssum: worth beyond beauty

Aster: delicate love

Azalea: romance

Basil: long-lasting love

Bay leaf: fame

Carnation: happiness

Chamomile: wisdom

Cherry blossom: feminine power and beauty

Chive: good luck

Chrysanthemum: optimism

Clary sage: elation

Clover: promise

Cranesbill: constancy

Daffodil: kindness and chivalry

Dahlia: elegance

Daisy: love and affection

Dill: good cheer

Evening primrose: silent love

Flax: gratitude

Forget-me-not: faithfulness

Forsythia: anticipation

Freesia: innocence

Gardenia: ecstasy

Hibiscus: delicate beauty

Hollyhock: all-consuming love

Honeysuckle: unity

Hyacinth: admiration

Hydrangea: devotion

Iris: passion

Ivy: everlasting love

Jasmine: heartwarming love

Jonquil: desire

Lavender: nurturing love

Lilac: innocence

Lily: beauty and loyalty

Linden: grace

Marigold: sacred affection

Narcissus: respect

Orange blossom: romantic love

Orchid: comfort and luxury

Parsley: merriment

Peony: renewal

Periwinkle: closeness

Petunia: reassurance

Rose: love

Rosemary: remembrance

Sage: wisdom

Sunflower: adoration

Sweet pea: long-lasting love

Tulip: devotion

Violet: purity, love, and peace

Wallflower: fidelity

Wormwood: requited love

Zinnia: happiness

THE PERFECT ROSE

The rose is perhaps the ultimate flower of love, representing romance, sensuality, eternal life, passion, physical perfection, and purity all in one. To ancient Greeks, the rose was the emblem of the goddess of love, Aphrodite. Romans believed a red rose first grew when love goddess Venus pricked her finger on a thorn and it bled on a white rose, turning it red.

Just as various flowers have different meanings, different roses have unique meanings.

Lavender: Enchantment, uniqueness

Orange: Fascination

Fuchsia: Gratitude, admiration

Red: Love, respect, and courage

Peach: Modesty, gratitude, admiration, but also sympathy

Pale Pink: Grace, joy, and happiness

Crimson: Beauty and passion

White: Innocence, purity, and reverence, but also secrecy, silence, and humility

Yellow: Joy, friendship, hope, and freedom, but also jealousy

A mix of red and white: Unity

A mix of yellow and orange: Passionate thoughts

A mix of yellow and red: Congratulations

Thornless roses mean love at first sight.

Tea roses mean you will be remembered always.

Just as rosebuds are themselves not fully grown, a gift of rosebuds stands for beauty, youth, and an innocent heart. Red rosebuds signify purity and loveliness, while white rosebuds are a gift best given to young girls.

THE POWER OF GEMSTONES
AND PRECIOUS METALS

Gemstones and precious metals have the ability to heal wounds, attract positive outcomes, and protect their wearer. If you receive jewelry as a gift, harness its power. And if you are giving jewelry, mix metals and gemstones for the most powerful effect.

Amber: changes negative to positive

Amethyst: calms the mind, brings clarity and wisdom

Aquamarine: brings courage and offers protection and strength

Carnelian: banishes envy and helps seize opportunities

Citrine: attracts success and wealth

Diamond: offers protection

Emerald: brings patience

Garnet: gives passion, constancy, stability

Gold: brings good health and willpower

Hematite: soothes and calms anxiety

Jade: offers serenity and prosperity

Lodestone: attracts love

Moonstone: amplifies feminine power

Onyx: brings stability

Opal: clarifies buried feelings and desires

Pearl: scares off sadness, brings joy

Peridot: brings understanding, acceptance; relieves fear and jealousy

Platinum: offers protection

Rose Quartz: draws love and passion, opens the heart, allows free exchange of love

Ruby: heightens self-confidence

Sapphire: increases insight, intuition, and communication

Silver: prompts creative juices to flow, ushers in prosperity

Tigereye: changes anxiety to confidence, motivation, and action

Topaz: brings on physical stamina and fidelity

Turquoise: creates a grounding presence, attracts prosperity

THE LEGEND OF
ST. VALENTINE'S DAY

Stories abound on how Valentine's Day came to be, but one version has it that the namesake of the holiday was a Roman priest named Valentine who lived in the third century. The emperor at the time, Claudius II, decreed that marriage was forbidden for young men, believing that single men made better soldiers than men with wives and families. As the story goes, Valentine defied the emperor and began performing marriages in secret. He was eventually discovered, jailed, and executed. But his legend persisted, and by the Middle Ages, Valentine had become one of the most popular saints in Europe.

In the fifth century, February 14 was declared St. Valentine's Day. Around this same time, the Roman "lottery" system for marriage (in which young men and women would pick the names of their future mates out of a hat) was abolished. Romance began to run rampant.

And then the valentining began. In Great Britain, Valentine's Day began to be popularly celebrated around 1600 C.E. And by 1750 C.E. or so, the practice of exchanging handwritten notes with friends and lovers had become common. By 1800 C.E., printed cards began to replace handwritten letters, and the ready-made valentine was born. In the 1840s, the first mass-produced valentines were sold in America.

The oldest known valentine in existence was written in 1415 C.E. by Charles, Duke of Orleans, to his wife, and is part of the manuscript collection of the British Library in London.

ANNIVERSARY GIFTS

The custom of giving gifts to commemorate wedding anniversaries began in medieval Europe, when a wife would be presented with a silver wreath once she had reached her twenty-fifth year of marriage. And on the fiftieth anniversary, she would receive a wreath of gold. These gifts stood for the rare and special love that must exist between the couple, given that their marriage had lasted so long.

This practice was elaborated upon, and now, in more modern times, most anniversaries are associated with a particular gift.

YEARS OF MARRIAGE	TRADITIONAL	MODERN	FLOWER
1	Paper	Clocks	Carnation
2	Cotton	China	Lily of the valley
3	Leather	Crystal	Sunflower
4	Fruit or flowers	Appliances	Hydrangea
5	Wood	Silverware	Daisy
6	Sugar or iron	Wood	Calla lily

YEARS OF MARRIAGE	TRADITIONAL	MODERN	FLOWER
7	Wool or copper	Desk sets	Freesia
8	Bronze or pottery	Linens or lace	Lilac
9	Pottery or willow	Leather	Bird-of-paradise
10	Tin or aluminum	Diamond jewelry	Daffodil
11	Steel	Jewelry	Tulip
12	Silk or linen	Pearls	Peony
13	Lace	Textiles or furs	Chrysanthemum
14	Ivory	Gold jewelry	Dahlia
15	Crystal	Watches	Rose
16		Silver hollowware	
17		Furniture	
18		Porcelain	
19		Bronze	
20	China	Platinum	Aster

YEARS OF MARRIAGE	TRADITIONAL	MODERN	FLOWER
21		Brass or nickel	
22		Copper	
23		Silver plate	
24		Musical instruments	
25	Silver	Silver	Iris
28			Orchid
30	Pearl	Diamond	Lily
35	Coral	Jade	
40	Ruby	Ruby	Gladiolus
45	Sapphire	Sapphire	
50	Gold	Gold	Yellow rose or violet
55	Emerald	Emerald	
60	Diamond	Diamond	
70	Platinum	Platinum	

SYMBOLS OF LOVE

These items can make wonderful (if sometimes unexpected) gifts of love.

APPLE

Before the apple came to represent temptation in the story of Adam and Eve, it stood for love, fertility, virtue, and abundance. Early Greeks would share an apple at their marriage ceremonies to bring forth happiness and fertility. The Greek god Dionysus gave apples to Aphrodite to try and win her love. And at the wedding of Zeus and Hera, apples were on hand to symbolize long-lasting love. Finally, in Chinese tradition, the apple blossom signifies adoration, and in Celtic tradition, fertility.

DOVE

Doves are a long-standing symbol of peace, but also represent deep love. Doves mate for life, with one bird often unable to survive if the other dies—and thus signify loyalty and fidelity. In the Hindu tradition, the dove represents the infinite capacity the heart has for love. And in Greco-Roman mythology, the dove was the sacred animal of love goddess Aphrodite/Venus. And doves are often used in Western weddings to symbolize ongoing love of couples.

HARP

Celtic, Norwegian, and Icelandic traditions hold that the harp represents a bridge of eternal love that connects heaven and earth.

LOVE KNOT

The love knot is best known as a Celtic tradition. With no beginning or end, the knot represents eternal love. It was also used in ancient Muslim culture, when young women would send secret messages, hidden in knots of cloth, to their beloveds.

MAPLE LEAF

Maple leaves, placed at the foot of a couple's bed, will both keep demons away and bring on peaceful sleep. The maple leaf is also a symbol of lovers in China and Japan. Finally, the stork uses maple branches in its nest, making the maple tree a symbol that represents fertility in a couple.

RINGS

Rings, with no beginning and no end, have long been a tradition for consecrating marriages in the Western world. However, the first wedding rings appeared in ancient Egypt, where they represented eternity as well as the deities of the sun and the moon. The metals that rings are made from are not only durable but are also believed to have magnetic properties that trap and hold love.

ROSE

The rose represents pure romance and love. Ancient Greeks held the rose to be the sacred emblem of beauty of Aphrodite, the goddess of love, and according to legend, the red rose grew from the blood of the god Adonis. The rose is also associated with Roman deities Hecate and Bacchus, and the Three Graces.

SEASHELL

The seashell's hard outer layer represents the protectiveness of love. According to ancient legend, Venus, the Roman goddess of love, emerged from the sea and was ferried to shore, fully formed, on a scallop shell (as depicted in Botticelli's famous painting *Birth of Venus*). The Hindu goddess of beauty and fertility, Lakshmi, was also created from the sand and pearls within an oyster shell.

SWAN

The swan stands for love, grace, and beauty. Zeus, the king of the Greek gods, transformed himself into a swan to woo the mortal queen Leda. On the other hand, in Celtic mythology, swans are able to take human form to seek love. The swan also symbolizes purity and chastity: in this aspect, it has been associated with the Virgin Mary and with Aphrodite.

EXTRAVAGANT GIFTS OF LOVE

Love often knows no bounds, as these over-the-top demonstrations prove.

CATHERINE THE GREAT'S GIFTS

Catherine the Great ruled Russia for thirty-four years in the second half of the eighteenth century. Her gifts were legendary; it is estimated that she spent more than ninety-two million rubles on presents during her reign and in so doing left the country in massive debt after her death. One major recipient of her generosity was Count Grigory Orlov, a military commander and one of Catherine's many lovers. Her first gift to him, on her coronation day, was eight hundred serfs. She later built him a palace in St. Petersburg, containing thirty-two different kinds of marble. Finally, she bought him a country estate near St. Petersburg, as well as four villages that surrounded it, so he would have uninterrupted views wherever he looked. Orlov returned Catherine's generosity by presenting her with a 190-carat diamond he acquired in India, which she named "The Orlov" and had incorporated into a royal scepter.

CLEOPATRA'S CARPET

Around 48 B.C.E., Egyptian queen Cleopatra was forced from her throne by her brother Ptolemy and had to flee to Syria. She wished to regain power and realized that in order to do so she would need the support of Roman ruler Julius Caesar. She had her servants go to Caesar's palace and present him with a gift of a beautiful Persian carpet. The servants then unrolled the carpet to reveal Cleopatra herself hidden inside. Caesar was taken with this gesture and with the queen, and not only did she regain her throne with his help, she also became his mistress and allegedly bore him a son.

MARIA THERESA'S FUR COAT

Louis XIV, the Sun King of France, ruled for seventy-two years in the seventeenth and eighteenth centuries and during that time displayed his extravagant taste with gifts he lavished upon his two wives and many mistresses. One extraordinary gift was made to his first wife (and first cousin), Maria Theresa of Spain. It was a sable fur coat, with a train said to be nearly one mile long. Maria Theresa's servants would spread the train of the coat out before her, and she would then put the coat on and thus be able to take morning walks in the garden of Versailles barefoot.

THE TAJ MAHAL

In 1612, Emperor Shah Jahan of India married Mumtaz Mahal, a Persian princess. She bore him 14 children during their happy union. While on her deathbed, she asked Shah Jahan to build her a beautiful mausoleum to symbolize their love, where their bodies could both reside after death. Shah Jahan began construction and twenty-two years later, after the work of more than twenty thousand laborers and at a cost of eighty-three million rupees and thousands of tons of pure white marble, the Taj Mahal was completed and the body of Mumtaz interred there. Shortly thereafter, Shah Jahan was overthrown by his son and imprisoned in a fort across the river from the Taj Mahal, from which he could see the mausoleum. He spent most of his time staring at it until he, too, died and was buried alongside his wife.

THE TAYLOR-BURTON DIAMOND

In 1972, actor Richard Burton bid on a 69.42-carat pear-shaped diamond from South Africa at auction. He was outbid but managed to negotiate a six-figure deal with the buyer, the Cartier company, to acquire the diamond, under the conditions that the diamond could be displayed temporarily at Cartier stores in New York and Chicago. Burton then presented it to his wife, Elizabeth Taylor, as a gift for her fortieth birthday. In 1979, after her divorce from Burton, Taylor sold the diamond for five million dollars, and used part of the proceeds to build a hospital in Botswana, near where the diamond was originally mined.

Thy lips, O my spouse,
drop as the honeycomb;
honey and milk
are under thy tongue.

~Song of Solomon

Food does not only provide nourishment and sustenance.
It can also bring good luck in love! Choose your meals wisely,
and love will be yours.

FOODS OF LOVE:
APHRODISIACS AND
OTHER LUCK-IN-LOVE EDIBLES

The word *aphrodisiac* originated from a festival celebrating the Greek goddess of love, Aphrodite. Her worshippers feasted on a sumptuous banquet and afterward engaged in ritual sex acts with her priestesses—hence the concept of good food leading to good love.

ASPARAGUS

Asparagus is high in vitamin E, a hormonal stimulant. Eat asparagus for three days in a row for best results. The water in which asparagus has been boiled may also be consumed for increased sexual vitality.

BANANAS

Bananas are excellent sources of potassium and B vitamins, both necessary for the production of sex hormones.

BLACK PEPPER

Black pepper has energizing properties. It contains the compound piperine, which ancients believed could stimulate sexual function.

CHEESE

Cheese, especially aged cheese, is a harbinger of lasting romance.

CHERRIES

Cherries, both raw and cooked, augur successful love and an easy, happy relationship.

CHILE PEPPERS

Chile peppers increase the heart rate, stimulate nerve endings, and trigger the release of endorphins, creating a natural high that can lead to amorous activity.

CHOCOLATE

Chocolate increases the amount of serotonin in the body. It also contains theobromine, a stimulant. The Aztec emperor Montezuma drank 50 cups of chocolate a day to maintain his legendary sexual stamina.

CLOVES

Ingesting cloves stimulates the sexual organs; the aromatic fragrance of cloves also enhances a romantic mood.

DATES

Dates usher in fertility.

EGGS

Eggs bring good fortune of all kinds, especially when it comes to fertility.

GARLIC

Garlic brings protection from harm. Eat it if you and your mate see danger on the horizon.

GINGER

Ginger stimulates the circulatory system, and has long been used as an aphrodisiac. Its use is recommended in such love texts as the *Kama Sutra*.

GRAPEFRUIT

Grapefruit chases away bitterness and evil; eat it if a relationship is going through a rocky patch.

HONEY

The ancient Egyptians believed that honey cured impotence and sterility, as well as increased the libido. In Eastern traditions, a groom would eat honey on his wedding day, and couples would drink mead, a honey wine, for a month after they married (this was called the "honey month," which later became "honeymoon"). Modern medicine has proven that honey aids in stamina and is also connected to testosterone and estrogen production.

MINT

Mint's refreshing taste makes it an effective aphrodisiac.

NOODLES

Noodles represent longevity. The longer the noodle, the longer your life together as a couple.

NUTMEG

Nutmeg has been used as an aphrodisiac for centuries by Chinese women; in small quantities, it increases the libido. However, do not think more is better, in large doses nutmeg can act as a hallucinogen.

OYSTERS

Oysters are high in zinc and protein, and contain compounds that lead to the release of sex hormones. Casanova ate dozens of oysters daily to maintain his legendary sexual prowess.

PINE NUTS

Pine nuts contain zinc, an essential mineral for male vitality. They have been used for centuries in love potions.

ROSEMARY

Rosemary engenders faithfulness; it also increases blood flow and heightens sensitivity.

SAFFRON

Saffron speeds up the neurotransmitters in the brain's pleasure center, creating lust, especially for women. It also contains a compound called picrocrocin, which is said to cause erotic sensations.

TOMATOES

Red and voluptuous, tomatoes were known as "love apples" in nineteenth-century France.

VANILLA

The taste and smell of vanilla increases lust in both men and women. In Mesoamerican mythology, Xanat, the daughter of a fertility goddess, transformed herself into a vanilla plant so she could bring pleasure to a mortal youth she loved.

WALNUTS

Ancient Romans believed that walnuts were aphrodisiacs and threw them at weddings to wish fertility upon couples.

WHEAT

Wheat and grain are signs of fertility and good fortune in love.

SPICE UP YOUR LOVE LIFE:
HERBS AND SPICES FOR LOVE

Anise: builds fidelity

Basil: encourages love

Cardamom: creates lust

Cinnamon: attracts love

Coriander: brings serenity and peace in love

Ginseng: creates lust

Lemongrass: draws pure love

Lemon verbena: purifies love

Marjoram: protects against broken hearts

Parsley: brings love and purification

Sorrel: heals love's wounds

Turmeric: purifies tainted love

WEDDING FOODS

The traditional wedding cake has its origin in several traditions. Ancient Egyptians would bake small cakes of wheat and barley and break them over a bride's head to bring good luck and fertility to her.

Giving almonds (or Jordan almonds) as wedding favors stems from an Italian belief that a gift of five almonds brought health, wealth, longevity, happiness, and fertility.

The throwing of rice at a couple comes from a pagan ritual in which a new couple was showered with grain. It was believed that the fruitfulness of the seeds would translate into a prosperous and fertile marriage, and would also ward off evil spirits. Later, rice began to be thrown instead of grain.

RECIPES FOR LOVE

GINGER-HONEY FRUIT SALAD

This cool, light, and refreshing salad will get the libido going without weighing you down—perfect for a summer seduction.

Serves 4

- ½ cup plain yogurt
- ½ cup honey
- ¼ cup fresh-squeezed lime juice
- 1½ tablespoons grated fresh ginger
- ½ teaspoon salt
- 2 cups chopped peaches
- 2 cups seedless red grapes
- 1 cup strawberries, halved lengthwise

In a large bowl, mix together the yogurt, honey, lime juice, ginger, and salt. Gently stir in the fruit and mix to combine. Let stand for a few minutes, and then serve.

CARAMELIZED ONION AND PINE NUT PIZZA

Caramelized onion will add sweetness to your love, pine nuts will increase potency, and rosemary will keep you and your mate true to each other.

Serves 2 to 4

2 tablespoons butter
¼ cup olive oil, plus 3 tablespoons
1 pound onions, thinly sliced
1 tablespoon kosher salt
1 tablespoon chopped fresh rosemary
¼ cup pine nuts, toasted
Cornmeal, for dusting
Flour, for dusting
½ pound store-bought pizza dough
Parmesan cheese

Melt the butter and ¼ cup oil together in a large skillet over medium heat. Add the onions and salt and sauté until the onions are translucent. Add the rosemary and reduce the heat to low. Sauté until the onions are golden brown, 20 to 30 minutes. Stir in the pine nuts.

Preheat an oven to 500°F. Dust a baking sheet with cornmeal. Lightly flour your hands and a work surface and stretch the pizza dough into a round 10 to 12 inches in diameter. Place it on the cornmeal on the baking sheet. Brush the dough with the remaining olive oil, and top with the onion–pine nut mixture. Grate Parmesan cheese on top to taste.

Bake in the oven for 8 to 10 minutes or until crust is golden brown.

CHOCOLATE-CHILE CRÈME BRÛLÉE

The one-two-three punch of chocolate, chile, and vanilla makes for a sweet ending to your evening—in more ways than one. Serve at a dinner party and all your guests will go home happy.

Serves 8

3 cups whipping cream
1 cinnamon stick
1 dried ancho chile, stemmed and chopped
⅓ cup sugar
6 ounces bittersweet chocolate, chopped
½ teaspoon vanilla extract
6 egg yolks (reserve whites for another use)
8 teaspoons vanilla sugar (available at gourmet food stores)

Preheat an oven to 350 °F. Combine the cream, cinnamon stick, chile, and sugar in a heavy saucepan and bring almost to a boil. Remove from the heat. Remove and discard the cinnamon stick. Stir in the chocolate until melted and smooth. Stir in the vanilla.

Whisk the egg yolks together in a large bowl. Add ½ cup of the chocolate mixture to the egg yolks; whisk briskly so the egg yolks do not cook. Add the rest of the chocolate mixture to the yolks.

Divide the mixture among eight small ramekins. Place the ramekins in a heavy baking pan, and add boiling water to come halfway up the sides of the ramekins. Bake for 35 minutes or until custard is nearly set in the center. Remove the ramekins from the baking pan and cool completely.

Just before serving, sprinkle the top of each ramekin with a teaspoon of vanilla sugar; place under the broiler until the sugar caramelizes, about 2 minutes (watch to make sure sugar does not burn). Remove from the oven and serve.

WALNUT-BANANA LOAF

*This delicious breakfast treat can also lead to a morning seduction.
Bananas rev up sex hormones, chocolate is a stimulant, and
walnuts are a noted aphrodisiac.*

Serves 6

1 ½ cups plus 2 tablespoons all-purpose flour

1 teaspoon baking soda

1 teaspoon baking powder

¼ teaspoon salt

1 cup semisweet chocolate chips

1 cup walnuts, toasted and chopped

1 stick (½ cup) unsalted butter, at room temperature

1 cup granulated sugar

2 teaspoons cinnamon

2 large eggs

2 mashed ripe bananas (about 1 cup)

2 tablespoons fresh lemon juice

1 teaspoon vanilla extract

Preheat an oven to 350 °F. Butter a 9-x-5-x-3-inch metal loaf pan. Stir the first four ingredients together in a medium bowl. Combine the chocolate chips and walnuts in a small bowl; add 2 tablespoons of the flour mixture and toss to coat.

Place the butter in a large bowl. Stir together the sugar and cinnamon, and then cream the butter with the sugar mixture until fluffy. Beat in the eggs, one at a time. Stir in the bananas, lemon juice, and vanilla, and then stir in flour mixture until incorporated. Gently stir in the chocolate chip–nut mixture.

Spoon or pour the batter into the prepared pan.

Bake until a toothpick inserted into the center of the loaf comes out clean, about 1 hour. Let the loaf sit in the pan on a cooling rack for 10 minutes, and then turn out onto the rack and cool completely.

ROASTED ASPARAGUS WITH GARLIC AND LEMON

Garlic will keep away any other contenders for your mate's heart, while the aphrodisiac powers of asparagus ensure that romance lies ahead.

Serves 2

  2 garlic cloves, minced
  ¼ cup dry white wine
  2 tablespoons olive oil
  Juice of ½ lemon
  Salt and pepper
  1 pound asparagus, cleaned and trimmed

Preheat an oven to 450 °F. Combine the garlic, wine, olive oil, and lemon juice in a small bowl and whisk to combine. Season with salt and pepper. Arrange the asparagus in a single layer in a shallow baking pan; pour the wine mixture over the asparagus. Roast for 10 minutes or until the asparagus are tender when pierced with a knife.

SALMON WITH GRAPEFRUIT-AVOCADO SALSA

If you have had a spat with your beloved and are feeling low, try this recipe. Salmon contains beneficial omega-3 fatty acids for youthful energy. Grapefruit will banish bitterness from your heart. And the Aztecs believed avocados had aphrodisiacal properties.

Serves 2

    1 small pink grapefruit
    1 ripe avocado
    Salt and pepper
    Two 5-ounce portions salmon fillet, skin on
    1 tablespoon vegetable oil

Preheat an oven to 350 °F. Cut the grapefruit in half and scoop out the segments from each half using a grapefruit knife. Place the segments in a medium bowl, and squeeze the juice from the empty grapefruit halves into bowl. Cut the avocado in half, remove the pit, and cut the flesh into 1-inch chunks. Add the avocado pieces to the grapefruit segments and mix gently. Season with salt and pepper. Set aside to let the flavors blend.

Season the salmon with salt and pepper. Heat the oil in a large oven-proof skillet over medium-high heat. Place the salmon fillets in the skillet, skin-side down, and cook for 2 minutes or until the skin is crisped and brown. Turn the fillets over and cook for 1 minute more. Transfer the skillet to the oven and cook for 5 to 8 minutes, depending on thickness of salmon. To test for doneness, insert a fork into a fillet. If the fish flakes, it's done.

Remove the salmon from the oven. Place the fillets on plates and top with salsa.

My heart is like
a singing bird...
Because the birthday
of my life
Is come,
my love is come to me.

- Christina Rossetti

There are many ways to express your love—displays
of affection, gifts, home-cooked meals, exotic trips. But
oftentimes sweet words are what lovers really want to hear.
This chapter will get you started.

PENNING A PERFECT LOVE NOTE

From *Hill's Manual of Social and Business Forms:
A Guide to Correct Writing*, published in 1882.

LETTERS OF LOVE

Of all letters, the love-letter should be the most carefully prepared. Among the written missives, they are the most thoroughly read and reread, and the most likely to be regretted in later life.

They should be written with the utmost regard for perfection. An ungrammatical expression, or word improperly spelled, may seriously interfere with the writer's prospects, by being turned to ridicule. For any person, however, to make sport of a respectful, confidential letter, because of some error in the writing, is in the highest degree unladylike and ungentlemanly.

NECESSITY OF CAUTION

As a rule, the love-letter should be very guardedly written. Ladies, especially, should be very careful to maintain their dignity when writing them. When, possibly, in aftertime the feelings entirely change, you will regret that you wrote the letter at all. If the love remains unchanged, no harm will certainly be done, if you wrote with judgment and care.

AT WHAT AGE TO WRITE LOVE-LETTERS

The love-letter is the prelude to marriage—a state that, if the husband and wife be fitted for each other, is the most natural and serenely happy; a state, however, that none should enter upon, until, in judgment and physical development, both parties have completely matured. Many a life has been wrecked by a blind, impulsive marriage, simply resulting from a youthful passion. As a physiological law, man should be twenty-five, and woman twenty-three, before marrying.

HONESTY

The love-letter should be honest. It should say what the writer means, and no more. For the lady or gentleman to play the part of a coquette, studying to see how many lovers he or she may secure, is very disreputable, and bears in its train a long list of sorrows, frequently wrecking the domestic happiness for a lifetime. The parties should be honest, also, in the statement of their actual prospects and means of support. Neither should hold out to the other wealth, or other inducements that will not be realized, as disappointment and disgust will be the only result.

LOVE LETTERS

Some of history's greatest love stories have played out in love letters.

Abigail Adams to John Adams, December 23, 1782

My Dearest Friend,

... should I draw you the picture of my heart it would be what I hope you would still love though it contained nothing new. The early possession you obtained there, and the absolute power you have obtained over it, leaves not the smallest space unoccupied.

I look back to the early days of our acquaintance and friendship as to the days of love and innocence, and, with an indescribable pleasure, I have seen near a score of years roll over our heads with an affection heightened and improved by time, nor have the dreary years of absence in the smallest degree effaced from my mind the image of the dear untitled man to whom I gave my heart.

Napoleon Bonaparte to his wife-to-be, Josephine, just before their 1796 wedding

I wake filled with thoughts of you. Your portrait and the intoxicating evening which we spent yesterday have left my senses in turmoil. Sweet, incomparable Josephine, what a strange effect you have on my heart! Are you angry? Do I see you looking sad? Are you worried? My soul aches with sorrow, and there can be no rest for you, lover; but is there still more in store for me when, yielding to the profound feelings which overwhelm me, I draw from your lips, from your heart, a love which consumes me with fire? Ah! It was last night that I fully realized how false an image of you your portrait gives!

You are leaving at noon; I shall see you in three hours.

Until then, mio dolce amor, a thousand kisses; but give me none in return, for they set my blood on fire.

Ludwig van Beethoven to an unknown woman, July 6, 1806

My angel, my all, my very self—only a few words today and at that with your pencil—not till tomorrow will my lodgings be definitely determined upon—what a useless waste of time. Why this deep sorrow where necessity speaks—can our love endure except through sacrifices—except through not demanding everything—can you change it that you are not wholly mine, I not wholly thine?

Oh, God! Look out into the beauties of nature and comfort yourself with that which must be—love demands everything and that very justly—that it is with me so far as you are concerned, and you with me. If we were wholly united you would feel the pain of it as little as I!

Now a quick change to things internal from things external. We shall surely see each other; moreover, I cannot communicate to you the observations I have made during the last few days touching my own life—if our hearts were always close together I would make none of the kind. My heart is full of many things to say to you—Ah!—there are moments when I feel that speech is nothing after all—cheer up—remain my true, only treasure, my all as I am yours; the gods must send us the rest that which shall be best for us.

Your faithful, Ludwig

John Keats to his beloved, Fanny Brawne, March 1820

Sweetest Fanny,

*You fear, sometimes, I do not love you so much as you wish?
My dear Girl, I love you ever and ever and without reserve. The
more I have known you the more have I loved. In every way—
even my jealousies have been agonies of Love, in the hottest fit I
ever had I would have died for you. I have vexed you too much.
But for Love! Can I help it? You are always new. The last of your
kisses was ever the sweetest; the last smile the brightest; the
last movement the gracefullest. When you passed my window
home yesterday, I was filled with as much admiration as if I had
then seen you for the first time. You uttered half complaint once
that I only loved your Beauty. Have I nothing else then to love
in you but that? Do not I see a heart naturally furnished with
wings imprison itself with me? No ill prospect has been able to
turn your thoughts a moment from me. This perhaps should be
as much a subject of sorrow as of joy—but I will not talk of that.
Even if you did not love me I could not help an entire devotion
to you: how much more deeply then must I feel for you knowing
you love me. My Mind has been the most discontented and
restless one that ever was put into a body too small for it. I
never felt my Mind repose upon anything with complete and
undistracted enjoyment—upon no person but you. . . .*

Your affectionate, J. Keats

Juliette Drouet, French actress, to Victor Hugo, 1835

If only I were a clever woman, I could describe to you my gorgeous bird, how you unite in yourself the beauties of form, plumage, and song!

I would tell you that you are the greatest marvel of all ages, and I should only be speaking the simple truth. But to put all this into suitable words, my superb one, I should require a voice far more harmonious than that which is bestowed upon my species—for I am the humble owl that you mocked at only lately, therefore, it cannot be.

I will not tell you to what degree you are dazzling and to the birds of sweet song who, as you know, are none the less beautiful and appreciative.

I am content to delegate to them the duty of watching, listening and admiring, while to myself I reserve the right of loving; this may be less attractive to the ear, but it is sweeter far to the heart.

I love you, I love you, my Victor; I cannot reiterate it too often; I can never express it as much as I feel it.

I recognize you in all the beauty that surrounds me in form, in color, in perfume, in harmonious sound: all of these mean you to me. You are superior to all. I see and admire—you are all!

You are not only the solar spectrum with the seven luminous colors, but the sun himself, that illumines, warms, and revivifies! This is what you are, and I am the lowly woman that adores you.

Juliette

Nathaniel Hawthorne to his wife, Sophia, December 5, 1839

Dearest,

I wish I had the gift of making rhymes, for methinks there is poetry in my head and heart since I have been in love with you. You are a Poem. Of what sort, then? Epic? Mercy on me, no! A sonnet? No; for that is too labored and artificial. You are a sort of sweet, simple, gay, pathetic ballad, which Nature is singing, sometimes with tears, sometimes with smiles, and sometimes with intermingled smiles and tears.

Love Amore Amour Love Amore Amour Amor Love Amore Amor Love Amore Amour Amour Love Love Amour Amour

**Letters between Robert Browning and
Elizabeth Barrett Browning,
1845–1846**

To Elizabeth Barrett Browning:

> *. . . would I, if I could, supplant one of any of the affections that
> I know to have taken root in you—that great and solemn one,
> for instance.*

> *I feel that if I could get myself remade, as if turned to gold,
> I would not even then desire to become more than the
> mere setting to that diamond you must always wear.*

> *The regard and esteem you now give me, in this letter, and
> which I press to my heart and bow my head upon, is all I
> can take and all too embarrassing, using all my gratitude.*

> *Robert Browning*

To Robert Browning:

And now listen to me in turn.

You have touched me more profoundly than I thought even you could have touched me—my heart was full when you came here today.

Henceforward I am yours for everything.

Elizabeth Barrett Browning

WORDS OF LOVE

Sometimes it is not worth reinventing the wheel when professing your love. Draw love inspiration from these poets.

THE PASSIONATE SHEPHERD TO HIS LOVE

by Christopher Marlowe

Come live with me and be my love,
And we will all the pleasures prove
That valleys, groves, hills, and fields,
Woods or steepy mountain yields.

And we will sit upon the rocks,
Seeing the shepherds feed their flocks,
By shallow rivers to whose falls
Melodious birds sing madrigals.

And I will make thee beds of roses
And a thousand fragrant posies,
A cap of flowers, and a kirtle
Embroidered all with leaves of myrtle;

A gown made of the finest wool
Which from our pretty lambs we pull;
Fair lined slippers for the cold,
With buckles of the purest gold;

A belt of straw and ivy buds,
With coral clasps and amber studs:
And if these pleasures may thee move,
Come live with me and be my love.

The shepherds' swains shall dance and sing
For thy delight each May morning:
If these delights thy mind may move,
Then live with me and be my love.

LOVE SONNET XVII

by Pablo Neruda

I don't love you as if you were the salt-rose, topaz
or arrow of carnations that propagate fire:
I love you as certain dark things are loved,
secretly, between the shadow and the soul.
I love you as the plant that doesn't bloom and carries
hidden within itself the light of those flowers,
and thanks to your love, darkly in my body
lives the dense fragrance that rises from the earth.

I love you without knowing how, or when, or from where,
I love you simply, without problems or pride:
I love you in this way because I don't know any other
way of loving

but this, in which there is no I or you,
so intimate that your hand upon my chest is my hand,
so intimate that when I fall asleep it is your eyes that close.

SONNETS FROM THE PORTUGUESE 43

by Elizabeth Barrett Browning

How do I love thee? Let me count the ways.
I love thee to the depth and breadth and height
My soul can reach, when feeling out of sight
For the ends of Being and ideal Grace.
I love thee to the level of everyday's
Most quiet need, by sun and candlelight.
I love thee freely, as men strive for Right;
I love thee purely, as they turn from Praise.
I love thee with the passion put to use
In my old griefs, and with my childhood's faith.
I love thee with a love I seemed to lose
With my lost saints I love thee with the breath,
Smiles, tears, of all my life! and, if God choose,
I shall but love thee better after death.

TO HIS COY MISTRESS

by Andrew Marvell

Had we but world enough, and time,
This coyness, Lady, were no crime
We would sit down and think which way
To walk and pass our long love's day.
Thou by the Indian Ganges' side
Shouldst rubies find: I by the tide
Of Humber would complain. I would
Love you ten years before the Flood,
And you should, if you please, refuse
Till the conversion of the Jews.
My vegetable love should grow
Vaster than empires, and more slow;
An hundred years should go to praise
Thine eyes and on thy forehead gaze;
Two hundred to adore each breast,
But thirty thousand to the rest;
An age at least to every part,
And the last age should show your heart.
For, Lady, you deserve this state,
Nor would I love at lower rate.
But at my back I always hear
Time's wingèd chariot hurrying near;
And yonder all before us lie

Deserts of vast eternity.
Thy beauty shall no more be found,
Nor, in thy marble vault, shall sound
My echoing song: then worms shall try
That long preserved virginity,
And your quaint honour turn to dust,
And into ashes all my lust:
The grave's a fine and private place,
But none, I think, do there embrace.
Now therefore, while the youthful hue
Sits on thy skin like morning dew,
And while thy willing soul transpires
At every pore with instant fires,
Now let us sport us while we may,
And now, like amorous birds of prey,
Rather at once our time devour
Than languish in his slow-chapt power.
Let us roll all our strength and all
Our sweetness up into one ball,
And tear our pleasures with rough strife
Through the iron gates of life:
Thus, though we cannot make our sun
Stand still, yet we will make him run.

SHE WALKS IN BEAUTY

by Lord Byron

She walks in beauty, like the night
Of cloudless climes and starry skies;
And all that's best of dark and bright
Meet in her aspect and her eyes:
Thus mellowed to that tender light
Which heaven to gaudy day denies.

One shade the more, one ray the less,
Had half impaired the nameless grace
Which waves in every raven tress,
Or softly lightens o'er her face;
Where thoughts serenely sweet express
How pure, how dear their dwelling place.

And on that cheek, and o'er that brow,
So soft, so calm, yet eloquent,
The smiles that win, the tints that glow,
But tell of days in goodness spent,
A mind at peace with all below,
A heart whose love is innocent!

SONG: TO CELIA

by Ben Jonson

Drink to me, only with thine eyes
And I will pledge with mine;
Or leave a kiss but in the cup,
And I'll not look for wine.
The thirst that from the soul doth rise
Doth ask a drink divine:
But might I of Jove's nectar sup
I would not change for thine.

I sent thee late a rosy wreath,
Not so much honoring thee
As giving it a hope that there
It could not withered be
But thou thereon didst only breathe
And sent'st it back to me:
Since, when it grows and smells, I swear,
Not of itself but thee.

BEAUTIFUL DREAMER

by Stephen Foster

Beautiful dreamer, wake unto me,
Starlight and dewdrops are waiting for thee;
Sounds of the rude world heard in the day,
Lull'd by the moonlight have all pass'd away!

Beautiful dreamer, queen of my song,
List while I woo thee with soft melody;
Gone are the cares of life's busy throng,—
Beautiful dreamer, awake unto me!

Beautiful dreamer, out on the sea
Mermaids are chaunting the wild lorelie;
Over the streamlet vapors are borne,
Waiting to fade at the bright coming morn.

Beautiful dreamer, beam on my heart,
E'en as the morn on the streamlet and sea;
Then will all clouds of sorrow depart,—
Beautiful dreamer, awake unto me!

ON MARRIAGE (FROM *THE PROPHET*)

by Khalil Gibran

You were born together, and together you shall be forevermore.
You shall be together when the white wings of death
scatter your days.
Ay, you shall be together even in the silent memory of God.
But let there be spaces in your togetherness,
And let the winds of the heavens dance between you.

Love one another, but make not a bond of love
Let it rather be a moving sea between the shores of your souls.
Fill each other's cup, but drink not from one cup.
Give one another of your bread, but eat not from the same loaf.
Sing and dance together and be joyous, but let each
one of you be alone,
Even as the strings of a lute are alone though they quiver
with the same music.

Give your hearts, but not into each other's keeping;
For only the hand of Life can contain your hearts.
And stand together yet not too near together;
For the pillars of the temple stand apart,
And the oak tree and the cypress grow not
in each other's shadow

LOVE'S PHILOSOPHY

by Percy Bysshe Shelley

The fountains mingle with the river,
And the rivers with the ocean;
The winds of heaven mix forever
With a sweet emotion;
Nothing in the world is single;
All things by a law divine
In another's being mingle—
Why not I with thine?

See, the mountains kiss high heaven,
And the waves clasp one another;
No sister flower could be forgiven
If it disdained its brother;
And the sunlight clasps the earth,
And the moonbeams kiss the sea;—
What are all these kissings worth,
If thou kiss not me?

William Shakespeare is perhaps the greatest love orator of them all, as these sonnets on the following pages prove.

SONNET 18

Shall I compare thee to a summer's day?
Thou art more lovely and more temperate.
Rough winds do shake the darling buds of May,
And summer's lease hath all too short a date.
Sometime too hot the eye of heaven shines,
And often is his gold complexion dimmed;
And every fair from fair sometime declines,
By chance, or nature's changing course untrimmed.
But thy eternal summer shall not fade
Nor lose possession of that fair thou ow'st;
Nor shall death brag thou wand'rest in his shade,
When in eternal lines to time thou grow'st,
So long as men can breathe or eyes can see,
So long lives this, and this gives life to thee.

SONNET 55

Not marble, nor the gilded monuments
Of princes, shall outlive this powerful rhyme;
But you shall shine more bright in these contents
Than unswept stone, besmeared with sluttish time.
When wasteful war shall statues overturn,
And broils root out the work of masonry,
Nor Mars his sword nor war's quick fire shall burn
The living record of your memory.
'Gainst death and all-oblivious enmity
Shall you pace forth; your praise shall still find room
Even in the eyes of all posterity
That wear this world out to the ending doom.
So, till the judgment that yourself arise,
You live in this, and dwell in lovers' eyes.

SONNET 109

O, never say that I was false of heart,
Though absence seemed my flame to qualify.
As easy might I from my self depart
As from my soul which in thy breast doth lie.
That is my home of love; if I have ranged,
Like him that travels I return again,
Just to the time, not with the time exchanged,
So that myself bring water for my stain.
Never believe though in my nature reigned
All frailties that besiege all kinds of blood,
That it could so preposterously be stained
To leave for nothing all thy sum of good;
For nothing this wide universe I call
Save thou, my rose, in it thou art my all.

SONNET 116

Let me not to the marriage of true minds
Admit impediments; love is not love
Which alters when it alteration finds,
Or bends with the remover to remove:
O, no, it is an ever-fixèd mark,
That looks on tempests and is never shaken;
It is the star to every wand'ring bark,
Whose worth's unknown, although his height be taken.
Love's not Time's fool, though rosy lips and cheeks
Within his bending sickle's compass come;
Love alters not with his brief hours and weeks,
But bears it out even to the edge of doom.
If this be error and upon me proved,
I never writ, nor no man ever loved.

SONNET 133

Beshrew that heart that makes my heart to groan
For that deep wound it gives my friend and me!
Is't not enough to torture me alone,
But slave to slavery my sweet'st friend must be?
Me from my self thy cruel eye hath taken,
And my next self thou harder hast engrossed.
Of him, myself, and thee I am forsaken—
A torment thrice threefold thus to be crossed.
Prison my heart in thy steel bosom's ward,
But then my friend's heart let my poor heart bail;
Whoe'er keeps me, let my heart be his guard,
Thou canst not then use rigour in my jail.
And yet thou wilt; for I, being pent in thee,
Perforce am thine, and all that is in me.

Love rules the court,
the camp, the grove,
And men below,
and saints above;
For love is heaven,
and heaven is love.

– Sir Walter Scott

Love is a universal emotion, yet it is expressed
in many different ways throughout the world.
Read on for new ideas about how to show your love.

50 WAYS TO LOVE YOUR LOVER

The three words "I love you" are among the most powerful in the English language. Expand your repertoire with 50 more ways to say "I love you."

Afrikaans: Ek het jou lief

Arabic: Nhebuk

Armenian: Yes kez sirumem

Bulgarian: Obicham te

Cambodian: Soro lan nee ah

Chinese (Cantonese): Ngo oi ney a

Chinese (Mandarin): Wo ai ni

Croatian: Volim te

Czech: Miluji te

Danish: Jeg elsker dig

Dutch: Ik hou van jou

Farsi: Doset daram

Filipino: Mahal kita

Finnish: Mina rakastan sinua

French: Je t'aime

German: Ich liebe dich

Greek: S'agapo

Hawaiian: Aloha au ia 'oe

Hebrew: Ani ohev otcha (said to a male)

Ani ohev otach (said to a female)

Hindi: Mai tumase pyar karati hun (said to a male)

Mai tumase pyar karata hun (said to a female)

Hungarian: Szeretlek

Icelandic: Eg elska tig

Indonesian: Saya cinta padamu

Irish: Taim ingra leat

Italian: Ti amo

Japanese: Ai-shiteru

Korean: Tangsinul sarang hayo

Lebanese: Bahibak

Malay: Saya cintakan mu

Moroccan: Ana moajaba bik

Norwegian: Jeg elsker deg

Polish: Kocham chebye

Portuguese: Eu te amo

Russian: Ya tebya liubliu

Serbian: Volim te

Spanish: Te quiero

Swahili: Ninapenda wewe

Swedish: Jag alskar dig

Tagalog: Mahal kita

Tamil: Nan unnai kathalikaraen

Thai: Chan rak khun (said to a male)

     Phom rak khun (said to a female)

Tunisian: Ha eh bak

Turkish: Seni seviyorum

Ukrainian: Ya tebe kahayu

Urdu: Me aap say pyaar karta hoo

Vietnamese: Em yeu anh

Yiddish: Ikh hob dikh lib

TERMS OF ENDEARMENT

Saying "I love you" is always good, but many couples take it further with special pet names and phrases for one another. Here are some notable examples from other languages.

Arabic
nur 'eyni: "the light of my eye"

Dutch
mijn schat: "my treasure"

Egyptian
azizi: "precious"

French
mon cochon: "my pig"
ma crotte: "my dropping"
ma puce: "my flea"
mon petit chou: "my little cabbage"
mon sucre d'orge: "my barley sugar"

Italian
cucciola mia: "my young animal"

Japanese

ichigo: "strawberry"

Norwegian

skatten min: "my treasure"

Polish

zabko: "froggie"

misiu: "teddy bear"

mam pociag do ciebie: "I am catching a train toward you"

Portuguese

meu gatinho: "my little cat"

Russian

solnyshko moyo: "my sun"

zaichik: "bunny"

Spanish

mi caramelo: "my caramel"

mi media naranja: "my orange half"

VALENTINE'S DAY
AROUND THE WORLD

America's most famous day of love is Valentine's Day. While many cultures and countries also celebrate this day, others have unique and different love holidays.

BRAZIL

Dia dos Namorados (Boyfriends' and Girlfriends' Day) occurs on June 12. On and around this day, single women perform rituals called *simpatias*, which they hope will help them find a boyfriend or husband.

ENGLAND

In Norfolk, the legend surrounding Valentine's Day is that a character called Jack Valentine knocks on the back door of houses on February 14 and leaves gifts and sweets for children.

FINLAND

The Finns celebrate *Ystavanpaiva* ("Friends' Day"), and this holiday focuses on remembering and doing nice things for all one's friends, not just romantic partners.

GUATEMALA

Guatemalans also celebrate a day of friendship on February 14, *Día del Amor y la Amistad* ("Day of Love and Friendship"). And as the name suggests, on this day people do nice things for their friends as well as their lovers.

JAPAN

On Valentine's Day, Japanese women give chocolates to men. One month later, on March 14, the Japanese celebrate "White Day," in which the men return the favor to women.

KOREA

The fourteenth day of every month is a love holiday in Korea. From January to December, they are Candle Day, Valentine's Day, White Day, Black Day, Rose Day, Kiss Day, Silver Day, Green Day, Music Day, Wine Day, Movie Day, and Hug Day. However, only a few of these are commonly celebrated.

ISRAEL

The fifteenth day of the month of Av (usually August) is the traditional Jewish festival of love. In olden days, girls would don white dresses and dance in vineyards on this day, and boys would watch them. Today, it is a popular date for proposing marriage.

PORTUGAL

Each April 23, the Portuguese celebrate St. George's Day, which they refer to as *Dia dos Namorados* ("Boyfriends' and Girlfriends' Day").

ROMANIA

Romania's holiday of love is called *Dragobete*, named after a character in folklore, and is celebrated on February 24.

SLOVENIA

A Slovenian proverb holds that "St. Valentine brings the keys of roots," and traditionally February 14 is the day when farm work commences after the winter. Only recently has it begun to be celebrated as a day of love; traditionally the Slovenian day of love has been March 12, St. Gregory's Day.

SPAIN

Those who live in Catalonia celebrate *La Diada de Sant Jordi* (St. George's Day) on April 23, and they give roses and books to their loved ones.

SWEDEN

February 14 is known as *Alla hjartans dag* ("All Hearts' Day"). It began to be celebrated in the 1960s, and sales of flowers on that day are exceeded only by flower sales on Mother's Day.

TURKEY

The Turkish day of love is called *Sevgililer Gunu* ("Sweethearts' Day"), and, inspired by Valentine's Day, is celebrated on February 14.

WALES

Dydd Santes Dwynwen (St. Dwynwen's Day) is on January 25 and commemorates St. Dwynwen, the Welsh patron saint of lovers.

WEDDING TRADITIONS AROUND THE WORLD

Worldwide wedding rituals and traditions are as unique as the countries themselves.

CHINA

A Chinese bride wears red at her wedding to symbolize the joy and love she hopes for in her life. At the wedding ceremony, the best man takes charge of a ritual involving the wedding rings, in which he takes the bride's ring and the groom's ring and places them on their fingers. He then places the bride's ring on the groom's finger, and vice versa, and then finally places them back on the correct fingers. This ritual symbolizes that when one member of the couple has weaknesses, the other will make up for it with strength, and vice versa.

ETHIOPIA

On the wedding day, the groom and several of his best men go to the bride's house, where her family and friends block their entrance as part of a ceremonial ritual. The best men sing songs to try and gain entrance to the house to see the bride. Once they are allowed inside, they spray the bride and the house with perfume.

FRANCE

In early French weddings, the bride would raise a glass of wine from one vineyard, and the groom, a glass of wine from another vineyard. The wine from both glasses would be poured into a third glass, and the couple would drink from that third glass. Oftentimes, a small piece of toast was dropped into the first two glasses to ensure a healthy life for the couple. This practice became known as "the toast"—and has endured until today. After the reception, guests would often gather outside the newlyweds' window and bang pots and pans, after which the bride and groom will invite them in for drinks in their honor.

GREECE

In Orthodox families, a celebration called a Krevati is held a few days before the wedding, in which family and friends place money and small children on the future marriage bed of the bride and groom, to bring prosperity and fertility into their lives. On the wedding day itself, the groom arrives at the ceremony before the bride. The best man takes charge of placing rings on the bride's and groom's fingers, and crowns on their heads. After the wedding, an odd number of candied almonds (usually 5 or 7) is passed out to guests.

INDIA

In the days before the wedding, the bride's hands and feet are adorned with elaborate henna designs. Family members also anoint the bodies of both bride and groom with a paste made of turmeric. On the day of the wedding, the bride wears red—never white, for white is the color of widowhood and mourning in India.

IRAN

At a Persian wedding, the mullah (Islamic clergyman) asks the groom if he wishes to marry the bride. The groom answers yes. Then the mullah asks the bride if she will accept the groom as her husband. She remains silent, while the wedding guests respond in unison, "The bride has gone to pick flowers." The mullah asks the bride the same question for a second time. Again, she does not reply, and this time her female relatives chant, "The bride has gone to bring rose water." The mullah repeats the question again and finally the bride answers in the affirmative—and then she and the groom are declared husband and wife.

IRELAND

Irish tradition holds that for good luck in married life, the following things must happen on a wedding day: the sun must shine on the bride, she must hear a bird sing on the wedding morning or see three birds in the sky, and after the ceremony, a man, not a woman, must be the first to wish the bride happiness. Newly married couples are often given a horseshoe with the ends pointing up to hang in their home, to catch good luck.

ITALY

In Italian wedding tradition, the color green is important and is believed to bring good luck to the couple—so the bride often accentuates her wedding-day ensemble with something green. Brides often also wear a veil, which ancient Romans believed would hide a bride from any evil spirits that were trying to hurt her. Bridesmaids wear dresses similar to the bride's to further confuse the same evil spirits.

JAPAN

Traditional Japanese bridal attire is a kimono, white face makeup, a wig, and a head covering. The bride and groom stay in separate rooms before the ceremony with their families. After the ceremony, the bride, groom, and their families perform a ceremony called *san-san-kudo* in which everyone takes sips from three cups of sake to symbolize the new bond formed between the families.

MALAYSIA

In Malaysia, the wedding ceremony spans two days. On the first day, the groom signs the marriage contract and agrees to provide the bride a dowry. Then both the bride's and groom's hands are dyed with henna, and the bride's hair may be cut. On the second day, the bride stays at her home with friends and family, and the groom sends small children there bearing gifts for her, which may include food, and origami flowers and birds made of paper money.

PHILIPPINES

It is considered bad luck for two Filipino siblings to be married in the same year. It is also seen as bad luck if the wedding rings drop to the ground at any point during the ceremony, and so the ring bearer is instructed to take great care. At the ceremony, wedding guests call forth prosperity for the new married couple by pinning paper bills to the groom's clothing and bride's dress during their first dance.

POLAND

Before a wedding, a groom usually goes with his parents to the bride's house, and both sets of parents give the couple their blessing. At the wedding itself, the bride and groom walk down the aisle together. They exchange rings, which they wear on their right hands, as part of the ceremony. After the ceremony, the couple and their guests travel to the reception—but on the way must go by "passing gates" that have been set up by wedding guests. In order to pass through, the bride and groom give gifts of vodka to those who guard the "gates." As they arrive at the reception, the couple's parents present them with bread and salt—bread to symbolize prosperity, and salt to symbolize the hardship of life.

ROMANIA

In Romanian tradition, the wedding ceremony includes singing and dancing that lasts all night. Just as dawn begins to break, the bride sits in a chair and is given a baby to hold for a few minutes, symbolizing the future children she will have. Her husband then takes her to their home and just before they cross the threshold, wedding guests shower them with grain to signify their future prosperity.

RUSSIA

A traditional Russian wedding can go on for anywhere from two days to a week, with the ceremony taking place on the first day and continuing with food and drinks, toasts, singing, and dancing. At any point during the wedding, if the guests begin chanting the word *gorko*, meaning "bitter," the bride and groom must embrace and kiss—this symbolizes that their love will keep bad things away throughout their lives.

After the wedding ceremony, the bride and groom race to see who will be the first to reach a white rug placed some distance away. Whoever steps on it first is said to be the master of the future household.

SCOTLAND

The groom and groomsmen traditionally wear kilts on the wedding day. The groom presents the bride with a silver teaspoon as a wish that they will never go hungry together, and he wears a sprig of white heather in his buttonhole for good luck throughout the marriage.

But love me
for love's sake,
that evermore
Thou mayst love on,
through love's eternity.

— Elizabeth Barrett Browning

Once you have fallen in love, you will want to know how to stay in love—forever. Whether it's the undying passion shared by star-crossed lovers in mythology, the stories of real-life true love, or time-honored tips on making love last, take inspiration from this chapter.

STAR-CROSSED
LOVERS OF MYTHOLOGY

PYRAMUS AND THISBE

Pyramus was the finest youth in all Babylonia, and Thisbe the fairest maiden. They lived in adjoining houses and were forced to communicate through a crack in the wall because their parents opposed their relationship. One day they decided they could take the separation no more and plotted to meet the next night, after sundown, by a stream lined with white mulberry trees. On the appointed evening, Thisbe stole from her house under cover of night, her face hidden by a veil. As she reached the meeting point, she saw a lioness approaching, so she quickly fled, dropping her veil in the process. The lioness took the veil up in her bloody jaws but soon abandoned it. When Pyramus came upon the scene, he saw the bloody veil and, assuming the worst, fell upon his sword. Thisbe returned to find him, and swearing never to live without him, took her own life as well. Henceforth, all the mulberries on the surrounding trees turned red and remain so to this day.

TRISTAN AND ISOLDE

Tristan was a Cornish knight, and Isolde, an Irish princess. Tristan traveled to Ireland to bring back Isolde for his uncle, King Mark, to marry. During the return journey both Tristan and Isolde accidentally drank from a potion that made them fall deeply in love with one another. They began an adulterous relationship while Isolde was married to Mark. Mark discovered their love, and Tristan was forced to leave the country. He traveled to Brittany and married another woman but never forgot Isolde. One day, he sent his wife's brother across the water to get Isolde back, telling him to return flying white sails if Isolde was with him, and black sails if she was not aboard. However, Tristan's wife forced her brother to lie. Tristan saw black sails and immediately died of grief. When the boat, with Isolde in it, reached shore, she found Tristan lying dead. She lay beside him, never to get up.

HERO AND LEANDER

Hero was a beautiful princess of Aphrodite who lived alone in a tower by the sea; Leander was a young Greek living just across the water. Every night, Leander would swim to Hero's tower, guided by a lamp she lit each night. In the morning, before sunrise, he would return to his home by swimming the opposite direction. In this fashion, they were secret lovers until winter came. One night, Leander attempted to make the swim to reach Hero, but a storm had come up and a fierce gust of wind blew out the lamp in Hero's tower. Leander could not see his way, and drowned. The next morning, his body washed up on Hero's beach, and when Hero herself saw him, she leapt from her tower to join him in death.

LAYLA AND MAJNU

Layla and Majnu were Indian youths who met in school. Majnu fell in love with Layla upon first sight and neglected his work because he was so smitten with her. The schoolmaster beat him for this, but every time it happened, Layla would be the one who bled. As they grew older, Layla and Majnu wished to marry, but Layla's brother Tabrez forbade it. In wild anger, Majnu murdered Tabrez. He was sentenced to be stoned to death, but Layla promised she would marry another man if only Majnu were spared. She did marry, but still pined for Majnu. When her husband realized this, he challenged Majnu to a duel. The two men met in the desert and drew their swords, and Majnu was pierced in the heart. At the same instant, Layla collapsed in her home and died. The two lovers were buried next to each other.

THE BUTTERFLY LOVERS

Zhu Yingtai was a beautiful and intelligent young girl but was not permitted to attend school because she was female. Thus, she disguised herself as a boy to fool the schoolmasters. While at school, she met fellow student Liang Shanbo and fell instantly in love, though he did not know her secret. Eventually Zhu left school and urged Liang to visit her at home so she could set him up with her "sister." When Liang did finally visit, he saw Zhu as her true self and fell instantly in love. However, it was too late: Zhu's parents had already arranged a marriage for her to someone else. Heartbroken, Liang fell ill and died. On the day of her marriage, Zhu's wedding procession traveled past Liang's grave. Zhu stood in front of it, and magically the grave opened. Still in love with Liang, Zhu flung herself into the grave. The spirits of the two transformed into a pair of beautiful butterflies, emerged from the grave, and flew together toward heaven.

FAMOUS STORIES OF TRUE LOVE

ABIGAIL AND JOHN ADAMS

Abigail Smith met John Adams in 1759, when she was fifteen years old. In the next few years, they began exchanging love letters (in a time when many women could neither read nor write) and were married in 1764. Theirs was an equal partnership, different from most marriages at the time; Abigail managed all aspects of their Massachusetts farm—planting, caring for livestock, managing staff—while John pursued politics. During the Revolutionary War, they continued to write letters back and forth. And when John was elected President in 1796, he relied heavily on Abigail's counsel in political matters. The couple was married for fifty-four years, until Abigail's death in 1818.

ANNE BANCROFT AND MEL BROOKS

Actors Anne Bancroft and Mel Brooks met when she was rehearsing her performance for a television show she was to be on. Brooks saw her on stage and was smitten; he bribed an employee of the show to tell him where she was going to dinner that evening so he could "accidentally" bump into her. Despite her being Catholic and him being Jewish, they wed in New York in 1964 and thus began a marriage that lasted forty-one years and was described as one of the happiest in the entertainment industry. Bancroft died in 2005.

ELIZABETH BARRETT BROWNING AND ROBERT BROWNING

Elizabeth Barrett was a well-respected Victorian poet by the time she met Robert Browning in 1845. He had read her book of poetry and, impressed by it, arranged a meeting with her. The couple courted for just under two years and in that time exchanged close to six hundred letters. They married in 1846 in England and then moved to Italy. There they both embarked upon an incredible prodigious period of writing, creating some of the greatest love poetry of all time, much of it based on their courtship, until Elizabeth died in Robert's arms in Italy in 1861.

QUEEN VICTORIA AND PRINCE ALBERT

Queen Victoria ascended to the British throne in 1837, when she was just eighteen. Prince Albert was her first cousin, a German, whom she first met in 1836. Despite opposition from her family, in 1839, she proposed to him, and they were married in 1840. Victoria relied on Albert in matters of state, and he proved a capable partner in this respect, and was a loving father to their nine children. When he died in 1861 of typhoid fever, Victoria was devastated. She withdrew from public life and did not appear in public for several years. She remained queen, but wore black for the rest of her life in Albert's memory until she too died in 1901.

MARIE AND PIERRE CURIE

Marie Sklodowska traveled from her native Poland to Paris in 1891 to attend college at the Sorbonne. There she met Pierre Curie, a budding scientist who courted her fervently until they married in 1895. They worked together on scientific studies, making major breakthroughs with the discovery of both polonium and radium. In 1903, they shared a Nobel Prize for Physics for their work in discovering radioactivity. Tragically, Pierre died in 1906 after slipping on a rainy street and being struck by a carriage. Marie took over his classes at the Sorbonne and forged on with their work. Until her death in 1934, she continued their scientific advancements, winning a second Nobel Prize. The Curies are buried together in the crypt of the Pantheon in Paris.

JOANNE WOODWARD AND PAUL NEWMAN

Actors Joanne Woodward and Paul Newman met in 1953 when they were both cast in a Broadway play. Newman was married at the time, but soon divorced, and five years later, he and Woodward married. Throughout their marriage, they appeared in several movies together, but stayed far away from the trappings of Hollywood, living in a farmhouse in Connecticut. When asked how he was able to remain faithful to his wife when he was an idol to so many women, Newman responded, "I have steak at home. Why go out for hamburger?" In January 2008, Newman and Woodward celebrated their fiftieth wedding anniversary. Newman died in September 2008.

HOW TO MAKE LOVE LAST

From *The Man and the Woman: Chapters on Human Life*, published in 1913.

The counsel that should be given applies to the period before marriages as well as to the years that follow. One of the great perils is in forming a wrong ideal, in expecting the wrong thing. We should have passed beyond the stage when young persons anticipate being "happy ever after" when once their union is sealed. Life is more of a piece than that; the old worries and trials may be exchanged, perhaps, for new ones, but worries and trials there will be to the end. Rightly shared, as in love they should be, they are a bond of union, not a dissevering influence. Without love they are fatal. No one must expect perfection, either in the character of the person to be wedded or in the circumstances of wedded life.

We are simply men and women after marriage as before; limited, faulty, liable to moods and tempers and depressions, but capable, also, with a little wisdom and patience, of living together in love that may be checkered, but should never be extinguished. Mere passion may die, but impassioned love not always, and calm love never.

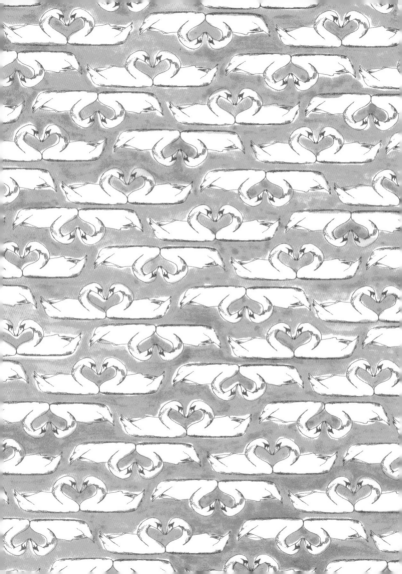